REFLECTIONS
FOR
ADVENT

2 – 28 December 2019

JAN McFARLANE
ANGELA TILBY

with an introduction to Advent
by LIBBY LANE

Church House Publishing
Church House
Great Smith Street
London SW1P 3AZ

ISBN 978 1 78140 133 0

Published 2019 by Church House Publishing
Copyright © The Archbishops' Council 2019

The opinions expressed in this book are those of the
authors and do not necessarily reflect the official policy of
the General Synod or The Archbishops' Council of the
Church of England.

Liturgical editor: Peter Moger
Series editor: Hugh Hillyard-Parker
Designed and typeset by Hugh Hillyard-Parker
Copy edited by Ros Connelly
Printed and bound by CPI Group (UK) Ltd, Croydon, CR0 4YY

What do you think of *Reflections for Daily Prayer*?

We'd love to hear from you – simply email us at

publishing@churchofengland.org

or write to us at

Church House Publishing, Church House,
Great Smith Street, London SW1P 3AZ.

Visit **www.dailyprayer.org.uk** for more
information on the *Reflections* series, ordering
and subscriptions.

Contents

About *Reflections for Advent*

Based on the *Common Worship Lectionary* readings for Morning Prayer, these daily reflections are designed to refresh and inspire times of personal prayer. The aim is to provide rich, contemporary and engaging insights into Scripture.

Each page lists the Lectionary readings for the day, with the main psalms for that day highlighted in **bold**. The collect of the day – either the *Common Worship* collect or the shorter additional collect – is also included.

For those using this book in conjunction with a service of Morning Prayer, the following conventions apply: a psalm printed in parentheses is omitted if it has been used as the opening canticle at that office; a psalm marked with an asterisk may be shortened if desired.

A short reflection is provided on either the Old or New Testament reading. Popular writers, experienced ministers, biblical scholars and theologians have contributed to this series, bringing their own emphases, enthusiasms and approaches to biblical interpretation.

Regular users of Morning Prayer and *Time to Pray* (from *Common Worship: Daily Prayer*) and anyone who follows the Lectionary for their regular Bible reading will benefit from the rich variety of traditions represented in these stimulating and accessible pieces.

This volume also includes both a simple form of *Common Worship* Morning Prayer (see pp. 34–5) and a short form of Night Prayer – also known as Compline – (see pp. 38–41), particularly for the benefit of those readers who are new to the habit of the Daily Office or for any reader while travelling.

About the authors

Stephen Cottrell is the Bishop of Chelmsford and before this was Bishop of Reading. He has worked in parishes in London, Chichester, and Huddersfield and as Pastor of Peterborough Cathedral. He is a well-known writer and speaker on evangelism, spirituality and catechesis. His best-selling *How to Pray* (CHP) and *How to Live* (CHP) have recently been reissued.

Libby Lane is the Bishop of Derby. In 2015 she was consecrated as Bishop of Stockport, the Church of England's first woman bishop. She chaired the Diocese of Chester Board of Education and the Foxhill Retreat House. She is Chair of Cranmer Hall Theological College Committee and Vice Chair of The Children's Society.

Jan McFarlane is the Bishop of Repton in the Diocese of Derby. She has served as Archdeacon of Norwich, Director of Communications, Chaplain to the Bishop of Norwich, Chaplain of Ely Cathedral and Curate in the Stafford Team Ministry.

Angela Tilby is a Canon Emeritus of Christ Church Cathedral, Oxford. Prior to that she served in the Diocese of Oxford following a period in Cambridge, where she was at Westcott House and St Bene't's Church. Before ordination she was a producer for the BBC, and she still broadcasts regularly.

Rachel Treweek is the Bishop of Gloucester and the first female diocesan bishop in England. She served in two parishes in London and was Archdeacon of Northolt and later Hackney. Prior to ordination she was a speech and language therapist and is a trained practitioner in conflict transformation.

Advent: a season of desire and danger

We try to make Advent visible in our household: we garland the fireplaces and stairs but decorate the foliage gently in purple; each Sunday we light a candle on an Advent wreath; we put up the traditional pine or spruce, but until Christmas Eve it is a Jesse Tree, softly lit, hung daily with simple olive wood images depicting salvation history through the stories of God's people in the Bible. These are outward reminders to us that the season of Advent is not simply a countdown to turkey and tinsel.

It's not that I think we just ought to replace one kind of outward display with another, more pious one. And I'm not a grinch. I enjoy the hospitality of the run-up to Christmas – I spend happy hours preparing stuffings and sauces to accompany our roast dinner. I admire the ways people find time and resource to focus on family and friends – I'm not very good at present-finding, but my (now grown-up) children have the knack of identifying often small, inexpensive or home-made gifts that are just right and show an attentiveness that is not only turned on for Christmas. These things can also be outward reminders of important and precious things – of love and hope and desire.

But the season of Advent demands inner work to find real truth under these outward displays. Although I say the Daily Prayers of the Church of England regularly, and find that rhythm and discipline valuable for my own walk with God and vital in maintaining my sense of belonging to the wider Church, Advent is one of seasons of the year when I find my desire to be drawn closer to God grows. The reflections in this book are a resource for the inner work of Advent.

Advent should be full of desire: 'come, Lord Jesus ... even so, come'.

That desire is, I think, wonderfully subversive. This season, if taken seriously, strips away all self-reliance and undercuts our hubris. If we allow it to, the eternal hopeful themes of the season can reveal the lack of substance in the relentless consumerism of the public face of the approach to Christmas.

Amid all the noise and activity of December, Advent is the thundering silence of God, putting all our striving to shame, reminding us that we cannot save ourselves or, in the end, hide from God.

Advent is an arrival not an avoidance, a facing up to the truth, a confronting of 'big' things – death, judgement, heaven and hell. Advent requires that we look backwards, and forwards, and inwards. Advent is an asking to see God face to face.

It is, therefore, a momentous, seismic season. A season of daring that passes largely unnoticed now. Entering into this season risks everything. It offers a perspective that reverses and upturns the views we too easily accept. It takes courage to journey through Advent. There is no hiding, no wrapping the truth up with ribbon and baubles. Advent cannot be domesticated or infantilized.

Advent is full of contradiction: knowing all has been fulfilled, we nonetheless yearn with anticipation. And, I think, the extraordinary, outrageous mercy of Advent is the discovery that, as we yearn for Christ's coming – in both humility and glory – we discover that God has always risked trusting the outworking of salvation to the stuff of creation and to human flesh.

Advent challenges us to trust ourselves as much as God trusts us.

In his poem 'Annunciation' from *Walking backwards to Christmas*, Bishop Stephen Cottrell wrote about the danger of a lack of trust. I leave you with the words of that poem and pray that the reflections in this book encourage you, this season of Advent, to dare to trust:

> There is only one thing that prevents
> The gentle movement, heaven into earth:
> Not the fear that godly greeting brings,
> Nor cold presumption (God could never speak),
> Nor empty tomb, nor barren heart,
> Nor eyes searching, voices how long blaze,
> Nor the silence where there should be praise,
> Nor the bitter taste of human failing:
> But the lack of trust that what was promised
> Might in human flesh be born, achieved,
> How happy she who for us all believed,
> Strength of God in human weakness blending,
> Tenderly the humble servant lifted,
> From foetal cry the fatal mending.

+Libby Lane

Building daily prayer into daily life

In our morning routines, there are many tasks we do without giving much thought to them, and others that we do with careful attention. Daily prayer and Bible reading is a strange mixture of these. These are disciplines (and gifts) that we as Christians should have in our daily pattern, but they are not tasks to be ticked off. Rather they are a key component of our developing relationship with God. In them is *life* – for the fruits of this time are to be lived out by us – and to be most fruitful, the task requires both purpose and letting go.

In saying a daily office of prayer, we make the deliberate decision to say 'yes' to spending time with God – the God who is always with us. In prayer and attentive reading of the Scriptures, there is both a conscious entering into God's presence and a 'letting go' of all we strive to control: both are our acknowledgement that it is God who is God.

> *... come into his presence with singing ...*
>
> *Know that the Lord is God.*
> *It is he that has made us, and we are his;*
> *we are his people, and the sheep of his pasture.*
>
> *Enter his gates with thanksgiving...*
>
> (Psalm 100, a traditional Canticle at Morning Prayer)

If we want a relationship with someone to deepen and grow, we need to spend time with that person. It can be no surprise that the same is true between us and God.

In our daily routines, I suspect that most of us intentionally look in the mirror; occasionally we might see beyond the surface of our external reflection and catch a glimpse of who we truly are. For me, a regular pattern of daily prayer and Bible reading is like a hard look in a clean mirror: it gives a clear reflection of myself, my life and the world in which I live. But it is more than that, for in it I can also see the reflection of God who is most clearly revealed in Jesus Christ and present with us now in the Holy Spirit.

This commitment to daily prayer is about our relationship with the God who is love. St Paul, in his great passage about love, speaks of now seeing 'in a mirror, dimly' but one day seeing face to face: 'Now I know only in part; then I will know fully, even as I have been fully known' (1 Corinthians 13.12). Our daily prayer is part of that seeing in a mirror dimly, and it is also part of our deep yearning for an ever-clearer vision of our God. As we read Scripture, the past and the future converge in the present moment. We hear words from long ago – some of which can appear strange and confusing – and yet, the Holy Spirit is living and active in the present. In this place of relationship and revelation, we open ourselves to the possibility of being changed, of being reshaped in a way that is good for us and all creation.

It is important that the words of prayer and Scripture should penetrate deep within rather than be a mere veneer. A quiet location is therefore a helpful starting point. For some, domestic circumstances or daily schedule make that difficult, but it is never impossible to become more fully present to God. The depths of our being can still be accessed no matter the world's clamour and activity. An awareness of this is all part of our journey from a false sense of control to a place of letting go, to a place where there is an opportunity for transformation.

Sometimes in our attention to Scripture, there will be connection with places of joy or pain; we might be encouraged or provoked or both. As we look and see and encounter God more deeply, there will be thanksgiving and repentance; the cries of our heart will surface as we acknowledge our needs and desires for ourselves and the world. The liturgy of Morning Prayer gives this voice and space.

I find it helpful to begin Morning Prayer by lighting a candle. This marks my sense of purpose and my acknowledgement of Christ's presence with me. It is also a silent prayer for illumination as I prepare to be attentive to what I see in the mirror, both of myself and of God. Amid the revelation of Scripture and the cries of my heart, the constancy of the tiny flame bears witness to the hope and light of Christ in all that is and will be.

When the candle is extinguished, I try to be still as I watch the smoke disappear. For me, it is symbolic of my prayers merging with the day. I know that my prayer and the reading of Scripture are not the smoke and mirrors of delusion. Rather, they are about encounter and discovery as I seek to venture into the day to love and serve the Lord as a disciple of Jesus Christ.

+ Rachel Treweek

Lectio Divina – a way of reading the Bible

Lectio Divina is a contemplative way of reading the Bible. It dates back to the early centuries of the Christian Church and was established as a monastic practice by Benedict in the sixth century. It is a way of praying the Scriptures that leads us deeper into God's word. We slow down. We read a short passage more than once. We chew it over slowly and carefully. We savour it. Scripture begins to speak to us in a new way. It speaks to us personally, and aids that union we have with God through Christ, who is himself the Living Word.

Make sure you are sitting comfortably. Breathe slowly and deeply. Ask God to speak to you through the passage that you are about to read.

This way of praying starts with our silence. We often make the mistake of thinking prayer is about what we say to God. It is actually the other way round. God wants to speak to us. He will do this through the Scriptures. So don't worry about what to say. Don't worry if nothing jumps out at you at first. God is patient. He will wait for the opportunity to get in. He will give you a word and lead you to understand its meaning for you today.

First reading: Listen

As you read the passage listen for a word or phrase that attracts you. Allow it to arise from the passage as if it is God's word for you today. Sit in silence repeating the word or phrase in your head.

Then say the word or phrase aloud.

Second reading: Ponder

As you read the passage again, ask how this word or phrase speaks to your life and why it has connected with you. Ponder it carefully. Don't worry if you get distracted – it may be part of your response to offer to God. Sit in silence and then frame a single sentence that begins to say aloud what this word or phrase says to you.

Third reading: Pray

As you read the passage for the last time, ask what Christ is calling from you. What is it that you need to do or consider or relinquish or take on as a result of what God is saying to you in this word or phrase? In the silence that follows the reading, pray for the grace of the Spirit to plant this word in your heart.

If you are in a group, talk for a few minutes and pray with each other.

If you are on your own, speak your prayer to God either aloud or in the silence of your heart.

If there is time, you may even want to read the passage a fourth time, and then end with the same silence before God with which you began.

+Stephen Cottrell

Monday 2 December

Psalms **50**, 54 *or* 1, 2, 3
Isaiah 25.1-9
Matthew 12.1-21

Isaiah 25.1-9

'Lo, this is our God; we have waited for him' (v.9)

This is a song of praise celebrating God's victory over his enemies. The context is a national crisis in which God's people are threatened by foreign aggression. The song hails the defeat of an oppressive city, though it is not clear whether this has actually happened or whether it is still hoped for. Either way, the song points forward to the ultimate victory, when God 'will swallow up death for ever'.

The Christian life should be a life of praise. Sadly, it is a common human tendency to moan about the state of the world and only to invoke God as a last resort, rather than living from a point of expectant gratitude. Anger and fear dominate so many of our immediate responses. But today's passage points to a response that goes beyond complaint or anxiety. It encourages us to anticipate actively God's intervention. Advent calls us to trust that there will be indeed be a time when tears end, that there really is a feast prepared for the hungry, that shame and disgrace do not have the last word.

Praising God for his final victory is not only a way of keeping our spirits up in difficult times; it hastens the day of God's coming. In that sense, praise is a subversive act; it draws God's future into the horizon of the here and now.

COLLECT

Almighty God,
give us grace to cast away the works of darkness
and to put on the armour of light,
now in the time of this mortal life,
in which your Son Jesus Christ came to us in great humility;
that on the last day,
when he shall come again in his glorious majesty
    to judge the living and the dead,
we may rise to the life immortal;
through him who is alive and reigns with you,
in the unity of the Holy Spirit,
one God, now and for ever.

| *Reflection by* **Angela Tilby**

Psalms **80**, 82 *or* **5**, 6 (8)
Isaiah 26.1-13
Matthew 12.22-37

Tuesday 3 December

Isaiah 26.1-13

'... all that we have done, you have done for us' (v.12)

'Thou wilt keep him in perfect peace, whose mind is stayed on thee.' Samuel Sebastian Wesley's 1853 setting of the King James' version of those words (v.3) is one of the most popular items in the choral repertoire. It suggests quiet steadfastness in the face of difficulty, holding on to faith in spite of challenging circumstances.

One of the central themes of Advent is that of waiting on God. But this waiting should not be interpreted as passive quietism. There is no point in achieving a private inner peace that is disconnected from outer events. Isaiah's prophecies were delivered in the midst of a series of national crises, the first of which was the threat from Assyria during the eighth century BC. Trusting God is not about personal serenity so much as a focused yearning for God to reveal himself. God has already delivered judgement. The end is not in doubt. Our task is to live bravely in the confidence that God has acted for us even though we do not yet see his will done on earth or even see clearly his will for our own lives.

We need to imitate the prophet in speaking of our future hopes in the past tense. God has already done what he promises to do; our task is to continue obediently to imagine God's future and praise him for it.

Almighty God,
as your kingdom dawns,
turn us from the darkness of sin to the
light of holiness,
that we may be ready to meet you
in our Lord and Saviour, Jesus Christ.

COLLECT

Wednesday 4 December

Isaiah 28.1-13

'... yet they would not hear' (v.12)

There are patterns in human history. Isaiah's message of steadfast trust in God during the Assyrian crisis struck such a deep chord that it was reapplied many times. The collection of oracles that form the book that bears his name is the result of a long process of reflection and reinterpretation.

We too need to learn to listen to God over and over again. As we do so, we realize that the human heart is so disposed to resist God that his message is as ineffective for us as if it were in a language we do not understand. Yet God continues to call.

Advent is a time of listening again to fundamentals. Christians have an awesome responsibility to bear witness to God's presence, especially at times like our own when the fear of God has vanished from public awareness. We need to realize that faith is more than a vague ethic of niceness. We should also be wary of simply accepting selfishness and corruption in society as though they were inevitable. What is wrong with us is not cured by wishful thinking; patterns of sin are only undone by deep change in the human heart. Reality comes from taking a step back and acknowledging our ultimate dependence on God. As Isaiah's hearers discovered, what we forget we are condemned to repeat.

COLLECT

Almighty God,
give us grace to cast away the works of darkness
and to put on the armour of light,
now in the time of this mortal life,
in which your Son Jesus Christ came to us in great humility;
that on the last day,
when he shall come again in his glorious majesty
	to judge the living and the dead,
we may rise to the life immortal;
through him who is alive and reigns with you,
in the unity of the Holy Spirit,
one God, now and for ever.

Reflection by **Angela Tilby**

Psalms **42**, 43 *or* 14, **15**, 16
Isaiah 28.14-end
Matthew 13.1-23

Thursday 5 December

Isaiah 28.14-end

'Listen, and hear my voice; pay attention, and hear my speech'
(v.23)

The prophet rails against the politicians of his time, who are seeking to forge a prudent, defensive alliance with their neighbour Egypt. This, he insists, is empty, a 'covenant with death', and shows the lack of faith in God that is the heart of their national crisis. The decision to turn against God means God can only be experienced as an enemy. The land is doomed to destruction. Yet God is still faithful to his promise; his precious cornerstone is laid in Zion and the 'one who trusts will not panic'. What is most needed is discernment, the recognition of how God is still at work among his people in spite of their lack of faith. God, like a wise farmer, is sowing seeds that will one day yield a rich, diverse harvest.

In 1934, T. S. Eliot's verse pageant 'The Rock' was staged in London. At a time of mounting political turbulence, perhaps not unlike our own time, Eliot invoked the God of Scripture and history and challenged audiences to remember their Christian heritage. This was a time of repentance and hope, to 'take no thought of the harvest, but only of proper sowing'. Whatever the future holds for us, what small deeds of 'proper sowing' should we be looking to do today?

Almighty God,
as your kingdom dawns,
turn us from the darkness of sin to the
light of holiness,
that we may be ready to meet you
in our Lord and Saviour, Jesus Christ.

COLLECT

Friday 6 December

Isaiah 29.1-14

'I will encamp against you; I will besiege you with towers' (v.3)

The politicians in Jerusalem have tried to do without God, and now God announces that he is about to fulfil their worst nightmares. God himself is to become the besieging enemy that they are terrified of. This passage has a dream-like quality as the prophet engages with the fears and fantasies that are enveloping his society, wound up by the experts and popular pundits of the day. Even the practice of faith has become formal and repetitive.

Today, we are so troubled by the thought of an angry avenging God that we are in danger of a new form of the old idolatry of making God in our own image. We cannot bear to think of judgement, or of the correcting chastisement of which the Bible speaks so frequently. Yet, and especially in Advent, we should perhaps be more ready to recognize how estranged we are from the living God. God's grace is a reforming, purging grace. He takes no pleasure in our perversity; his desire is always to bring wholeness and healing. But sometimes our wounds need to be made deeper before they can be healed. When our lives are suddenly struck by adversity and God becomes a stranger to us, we should try not to despair, but cling to the hope that the stranger is in reality our deepest, dearest friend.

COLLECT

Almighty God,
give us grace to cast away the works of darkness
and to put on the armour of light,
now in the time of this mortal life,
in which your Son Jesus Christ came to us in great humility;
that on the last day,
when he shall come again in his glorious majesty
    to judge the living and the dead,
we may rise to the life immortal;
through him who is alive and reigns with you,
in the unity of the Holy Spirit,
one God, now and for ever.

14   *Reflection by* **Angela Tilby**

Saturday 7 December

Isaiah 29.15-end

'The meek shall obtain fresh joy in the Lord' (v.19)

The society addressed in these prophecies was easily manipulated by rulers who believed that they alone had the savvy political skill to stave off disaster. The prophet suggests that in believing in themselves in this way they were acting as idolaters: substituting God's rule for policies of all-too-human origin. The people needed to look beyond the false wisdom of their current leaders to recognize that God's help was the *only* option that is grounded in genuine hope. Because the hope is grounded on an unshakeable promise, God's mysterious actions can be trusted, even in the present crisis.

It is all too easy in difficult times for everyone to look to their own interests and to ignore the common good. Anxious times can be an excuse for dishonesty as the rich and powerful seek to wield undue influence over those who make decisions. Yet from the standpoint of faith, the impending disaster is a spur to integrity, not an excuse for self-seeking.

As Advent progresses we should pray for a deep renewal of hope grounded in deep repentance. God still has hope for us even if we have little hope in God. As you reflect on this passage, notice where your own personal hopes are focused. What is your vision of God's grace for your own life today?

COLLECT

Almighty God,
as your kingdom dawns,
turn us from the darkness of sin to the
light of holiness,
that we may be ready to meet you
in our Lord and Saviour, Jesus Christ.

Reflection by **Angela Tilby**   15

Monday 9 December

Psalm **44** *or* 27, **30**
Isaiah 30.1-18
Matthew 14.1-12

Isaiah 30.1-18

'... the Lord waits to be gracious to you' (v.18)

The prophet's attack on Judah's proposed alliance with Egypt continues in this chapter. Determined that his witness will not be silenced, he records his testimony for future generations. He has come to realize that his advice is being rejected because exposing the illusions in which God's people are trapped is too painful for people to bear. But he does not his mince his words; relying on Egypt represents a rejection of God, and it makes his people far more vulnerable than they realize. While seeking support from Egypt, they are sitting on a time bomb.

All Christians share in the prophetic vocation of the Church. We are called to be watchful and alert at all times because we can all be seduced by false promises and seek a security that is not available to us. Christian discipleship in society means taking on something of the loneliness of the prophet; this is only possible if we consciously stay close to God, making time for prayer, study and trying as far as we can to maintain an untroubled spirit, 'in quietness and in trust shall be your strength ...'. Our febrile world seems both to expect catastrophe and to reject moral discipline. Our role is not to contribute to anxiety but to remain mindful of God, whose will for us is always gracious and just.

COLLECT

O Lord, raise up, we pray, your power
and come among us,
and with great might succour us;
that whereas, through our sins and wickedness
we are grievously hindered
in running the race that is set before us,
your bountiful grace and mercy
may speedily help and deliver us;
through Jesus Christ your Son our Lord,
to whom with you and the Holy Spirit,
be honour and glory, now and for ever.

Reflection by **Angela Tilby**

Psalms **56**, 57 *or* 32, **36**   **Tuesday 10 December**
Isaiah 30.19-end
Matthew 14.13-end

Isaiah 30.19-end

'This is the way; walk in it' (v.21)

In spite of the dire danger caused by the Assyrian crisis, the prophet points his people to the consistency of God's purpose for them. God's blessing outlasts his anger; his purpose is not defeated by the Assyrian threat. It is the enemy, in reality, who is courting disaster and will experience God's judgement. In the meantime, God does not abandon his people or cease to care for them day by day. The extreme circumstances they are experiencing are not at this stage a sign of God's judgement against them, but they are a real trial.

We tend to find the distinction between judgement and trial difficult to maintain. We somehow expect that God's care will show itself in ironing out our difficulties and solving our problems. We expect to be rewarded for our faith. But the reward of faith is not always experienced in the present, even in the course of our lifetime. We are often asked to shoulder long-term problems and uncertainties, bearing them in a spirit of trust and submission. It is through receiving 'the bread of adversity' and 'the water of affliction' that we learn to recognize and accept God as our teacher, Master and Lord.

Living with faith in the present moment means learning to live from a place of deep dependence on God, so that we become more and more sensitive to his voice.

Almighty God,
purify our hearts and minds,
that when your Son Jesus Christ comes again as
judge and saviour
we may be ready to receive him,
who is our Lord and our God.

COLLECT

Reflection by **Angela Tilby** | 17

Wednesday 11 December

Isaiah 31

'Turn back to him whom you have deeply betrayed' (v.6).

It is hardly surprising that those who have ceased to trust in God should seek refuge in the military might of a strong ally. In this chapter, the Lord reasserts himself as the Lord of history. Human beings cannot ultimately resist God's work in time; human weaponry is useless against the sword of God's spirit. For those living through periods of turbulence, Isaiah's message does not bring solutions to difficult dilemmas, but rather hammers home the message that it is only trust in God that brings true security.

We resist this because it seems to leave us with so many unanswered questions. The temptation is to rely on our own 'idols' of wealth and weaponry, or, as Isaiah's contemporaries did, on dodgy alliances with unreliable neighbours. There are many times in our own lives when we are tempted to betray the values of faith for greater personal security. This sometimes means compromising our Christian convictions to avoid conflict or unpopularity. Knowing this, we should always keep in our prayers our political leaders, who have to make decisions on our behalf. Sometimes it is impossible to make a 'right' judgement. But we can through prayer and witness keep the dilemmas of our time open to the workings of God's spirit, trusting that God will bring his ultimate purpose to fulfilment.

COLLECT

O Lord, raise up, we pray, your power
and come among us,
and with great might succour us;
that whereas, through our sins and wickedness
we are grievously hindered
in running the race that is set before us,
your bountiful grace and mercy
may speedily help and deliver us;
through Jesus Christ your Son our Lord,
to whom with you and the Holy Spirit,
be honour and glory, now and for ever.

| *Reflection by* **Angela Tilby**

Psalms 53, **54**, 60 *or* **37***
Isaiah 32
Matthew 15.21-28

Thursday 12 December

Isaiah 32

'The effect of righteousness will be peace' (v.17)

Isaiah longs for a righteous society, dependent on God, as the only security against disaster. He understood that nations often crumble from within before they succumb to attacks from without. So he presents the vision of a monarchy that is founded on justice and blessed by the outpouring of God's spirit. This is a development of other messianic prophecies from earlier in the book (Isaiah 9.6-7).

We should never forget that the Christian faith is good news for all humanity. The promises that take flesh in Christ are for the whole world. God desires a new humanity, free from the corruption of selfishness. He asks us to live the truth that we belong together, caring for the vulnerable and looking beyond our own interests. In addition, the peace that comes in the messianic age will see not only a virtuous community, but also a harmonious relationship with the natural world.

Advent is a time to examine ourselves for traces of the cynicism and complacency that hinder God's work, and are often an excuse for moral indifference. The Christian contribution is not to add to the noisy scepticism around us, or to withdraw into pietism, but to bear the struggles of the world before God, praying for his kingdom to dawn in power.

As we draw nearer to Christmas, let Isaiah's vision resonate with our anticipation of Christ's coming.

Almighty God,
purify our hearts and minds,
that when your Son Jesus Christ comes again as
judge and saviour
we may be ready to receive him,
who is our Lord and our God.

COLLECT

Reflection by **Angela Tilby**

Friday 13 December

Psalms 85, **86** or **31**
Isaiah 33.1-22
Matthew 15.29-end

Isaiah 33.1-22

'Your eyes will see the king in his beauty' (v.17)

'Everything,' said the French poet Charles Péguy, 'begins in mysticism and ends in politics'. Yet from a biblical perspective, the reverse is also true. Political crisis provokes prayer and a spiritual longing for a reality beyond the changes and chances of the present moment. We cry out to God, but in a sense God has already found us, and uses our fear and sense of urgency to draw out hearts back to him.

The oracles in this chapter reflect a national crisis. There is public mourning and widespread anxiety; travel is unsafe; there is a sense of deep betrayal. But none of this can destroy God's promise to his people, nor can it deflect those who remain faithful to God's standards in their everyday behaviour. The heart of hope is, as so often in Isaiah, vision – a vision of the future, but not confined to any single epoch or to any calculable future date. The king of verse 17 could be a messianic ruler, or even God himself. The point is that he is supremely desirable; we are drawn to him because he is so obviously the one our hearts long for.

Christianity knows no ultimate distinction between mysticism and politics. The orientation of mystical prayer is at one with the prophet's longing for justice and peace. Even so, come Lord Jesus!

COLLECT

O Lord, raise up, we pray, your power
and come among us,
and with great might succour us;
that whereas, through our sins and wickedness
we are grievously hindered
in running the race that is set before us,
your bountiful grace and mercy
may speedily help and deliver us;
through Jesus Christ your Son our Lord,
to whom with you and the Holy Spirit,
be honour and glory, now and for ever.

Reflection by **Angela Tilby**

Psalm **145** *or* 41, 42, 43
Isaiah 35
Matthew 16.1-12

Saturday 14 December

Isaiah 35

'... they shall obtain joy and gladness, and sorrow and sighing shall flee away' (v.10)

This chapter contains oracles that seem to reflect a prophetic ministry to people in exile rather than those involved in the original Assyrian crisis. But we have already seen how the collection of oracles that form the book of Isaiah recycle and reapply prophecies to meet changed circumstances. This passage provides a fitting climax to the fears and hopes we have encountered in previous readings. The general theme is restoration. There will be a triumphant return to a restored Jerusalem. Nature itself will help the returning exiles, providing a highway for their journey and water for their refreshment along the way. This is a time for courage and encouragement. God's salvation is at hand. The long wait is over.

As Advent progresses, the urgency of prayer is met by an increasing anticipation of joy. The wait will be worth it; the promised one is at hand. Advent is traditionally a time for meditating on the last things: death, judgement, hell and heaven. For Christians, the threat of death is answered by the hope that death itself is transformed by the coming of Christ. The long journey through this life is not a journey into nothingness but a pilgrim route to the city of God.

We should encourage each other and be encouraged as we wait the coming of the Lord.

Almighty God,
purify our hearts and minds,
that when your Son Jesus Christ comes again as
judge and saviour
we may be ready to receive him,
who is our Lord and our God.

COLLECT

Reflection by **Angela Tilby**

21

Monday 16 December

Isaiah 38.1-8, 21-22

'Set your house in order' (v.1)

Following a medical check-up, I grinned at the doctor and quipped, 'Not dying just yet then!' She glanced up from her desk and quipped back gently, 'We're all dying.' On one level, a light-hearted exchange. On another level, a sombre reminder of a universal truth. From the day we are born we are dying.

Isaiah can't have been looking forward to delivering God's message to Hezekiah. The king is to set his house in order because he's going to die. We're told he's just 39. He's in the prime of his life. It's not the news he's expecting.

The delivery of such a stark message may not have earned Isaiah top marks in pastoral care, but how often are we guilty of not talking openly about death with one another, and not even with those who know they are dying? We owe it to those who face a terminal diagnosis to speak honestly and truthfully, even as we listen carefully for clues that they are seeking such honesty. For in facing death openly, we can indeed 'set our house in order' and ensure that loose ends are tied up, unfinished business dealt with and broken relationships mended, before it's too late.

In Advent, we're encouraged to look towards the 'end times' and face our own mortality. What might you need to do today to ensure your house is in order?

COLLECT

O Lord Jesus Christ,
who at your first coming sent your messenger
to prepare your way before you:
grant that the ministers and stewards of your mysteries
may likewise so prepare and make ready your way
by turning the hearts of the disobedient to the wisdom of the just,
that at your second coming to judge the world
we may be found an acceptable people in your sight;
for you are alive and reign with the Father
in the unity of the Holy Spirit,
one God, now and for ever.

| *Reflection by* **Jan McFarlane**

Tuesday 17 December

Isaiah 38.9-20

'My dwelling is plucked up ... like a shepherd's tent' (v.12)

God grants Hezekiah a reprieve. He's in remission. Why do some people live and other people die? Why are some prayers answered and others seemingly not – or at least not in the way we'd like them to be answered? We've never really resolved that dilemma satisfactorily. Perhaps we must be content to live with the questions.

In celebration, Hezekiah writes a song. He reflects on the journey he has just been through and he knows that has been thoroughly changed by the experience. Like many of us who have known good health and prosperity, we can be lulled into believing we're invincible. But Hezekiah now knows how it feels not to be able to take tomorrow for granted. He feels like one who lives in a tent. It's a temporary structure, vulnerable to storms, fit for purpose for just a short while, and tomorrow it might be plucked up and moved on.

From now on, that is how Hezekiah will live these extra, all-too-precious, years of life. He now knows what it feels like to be called home to bed while his childhood pals are still out playing in the evening sun. He'll take nothing for granted. He'll live close to God and God's grace instead of trusting in his own power. He will indeed 'set his house in order'.

Might he even have seen that close encounter with death as a gift?

God for whom we watch and wait,
you sent John the Baptist to prepare the way of your Son:
give us courage to speak the truth,
to hunger for justice,
and to suffer for the cause of right,
with Jesus Christ our Lord.

COLLECT

Wednesday 18 December

Psalms **75**, 96 *or* **119.57-80**
Isaiah 39
Matthew 17.14-21

Isaiah 39

'They have seen all that is in my house' (v.4)

Hearing that King Hezekiah's health has been restored, the wily King Merodach-baladan sends the Babylonian equivalent of a get-well card and flowers, and sends envoys to pay a pastoral visit, bunch of grapes in hand. Hezekiah, flattered by the attention, welcomes them with open arms and innocently shows them around. The envoys' eyes must have nearly popped out of their head when they saw the wealth, the armour, the storehouses Hezekiah had amassed. The tiny kingdom of Judah was no match for the rising power and tyranny of Babylon. The writing was on the wall.

Hezekiah has many strengths. He has swept away all the pagan idols from his father's reign and initiated great religious reforms. He has trusted in God. He has walked in truth and with integrity. But his weak spot is common to us all. We are all, I imagine, too susceptible to flattery. It takes the straight-talking Isaiah to point out the foolishness of Hezekiah's actions. He has been too innocent, too open and too honest for his own good.

It seems strange to ask us today to consider whether, at times, we are too trusting, too open, too honest, too 'nice'. We know that we're taught by Jesus to be 'innocent as doves'. But do we sometimes forget, not least in church circles where we might innocently be flattered and even manipulated, that he also asks us to be 'wise as serpents' (Matthew 10.16)?

COLLECT

O Lord Jesus Christ,
who at your first coming sent your messenger
to prepare your way before you:
grant that the ministers and stewards of your mysteries
may likewise so prepare and make ready your way
by turning the hearts of the disobedient to the wisdom of the just,
that at your second coming to judge the world
we may be found an acceptable people in your sight;
for you are alive and reign with the Father
in the unity of the Holy Spirit,
one God, now and for ever.

| *Reflection by* **Jan McFarlane**

Psalms 144, 146
Zephaniah 1.1 – 2.3
Matthew 17.22-end

Thursday 19 December

Zephaniah 1.1 – 2.3

'Seek the Lord ... seek righteousness, seek humility' (2.3)

It's probably true to say that Zephaniah is not the best-known of the Old Testament prophets, so here is a quick résumé. Zephaniah describes himself as being of the line of King Hezekiah and is thought to be a distant cousin of the present king, Josiah. Egypt, to the south, is squaring up to Babylon in the north, and it's not looking good for Judah, caught between two of the greatest empires of the day.

Into this political maelstrom comes the voice of the prophet. He warns the people of Judah that, because they have turned away from the one true God and are worshipping other gods, they will be destroyed when the day of the Lord draws near. This is not what the people of Judah were expecting. They assumed God would save them on that mighty day. Not so, warns Zephaniah. There is only one hope, and that is for the people to turn back to God, to seek the Lord, to seek righteousness and humility.

As we look towards the day of the Lord in six days' time, will we be prepared to greet him? Or will we be distracted by the other Christmas gods of consumerism, advertising and the all-pervading god of busy-ness, which conspire to prevent us from seeking first 'the kingdom of God and his righteousness' (Matthew 6.33).

God for whom we watch and wait,
you sent John the Baptist to prepare the way of your Son:
give us courage to speak the truth,
to hunger for justice,
and to suffer for the cause of right,
with Jesus Christ our Lord.

COLLECT

Friday 20 December

Zephaniah 3.1-13

'... a people humble and holy' (v.12)

God's people remain hard-hearted. They don't return to the one true God, but instead continue to follow pagan gods and idols. Their leaders are corrupt and faithless. Zephaniah warns them that the surrounding nations will invade. It's all too late.

But there is still hope for those who wait for the Lord. God will give them 'pure speech', with echoes of a reversal of Babel and a hint of Pentecost for those of us who know the rest of the story. As we approach the Fourth Sunday of Advent, with its focus on Mary, the God-bearer, there are echoes here too of Mary's song. Zephaniah prophesies that God will bring down the proud and haughty and leave a people who are humble and holy.

Those who are saved will be a remnant. A minority. From the story of the Flood in Genesis right through to the end of the New Testament, the concept of 'the remnant' remains: those who return to God and become a sign of hope. Our churches this Christmas will be full. And after Christmas, the remnant remain. While it's important that we reach out to others with the good news of the gospel, it's important too that we don't lose hope when we remain a minority. In the words of the priest and writer, Sam Wells, 'Christianity isn't any less true just because it's less widely believed'.

Our calling is to remain faithful. A people humble and holy.

COLLECT

O Lord Jesus Christ,
who at your first coming sent your messenger
to prepare your way before you:
grant that the ministers and stewards of your mysteries
may likewise so prepare and make ready your way
by turning the hearts of the disobedient to the wisdom of the just,
that at your second coming to judge the world
we may be found an acceptable people in your sight;
for you are alive and reign with the Father
in the unity of the Holy Spirit,
one God, now and for ever.

Reflection by **Jan McFarlane**

Psalms 121, 122, 123
Zephaniah 3.14-end
Matthew 18.21-end

Saturday 21 December

Zephaniah 3.14-end

'The Lord, your God, is in your midst' (v.17)

Zephaniah's prophesy ends with a song of hope. Jerusalem will be restored. God will be in their midst as a warrior king. Three days away from Christmas Eve, we make the connection immediately. Here we have echoes of the incarnation. Emmanuel. God with us. The word made flesh moving into the neighbourhood. A king certainly, but one born in a humble cattle shed, not a palace. A servant, not a warrior.

In anticipation of what is to come, Zephaniah calls God's people to sing. They are to sing a song of hope because, while they can't yet see God's salvation, they must trust that it is very near. Singing in the midst of despair is an act of hope. A holy defiance. We trust that God will even yet deliver his promises.

Do you sing? Not just in carol services and formal worship, but on your own, in the car, around the house? Do you have a back catalogue of hymns, psalms and worship songs ready to strengthen and encourage you when you're down? Are you able to bring God's glorious future into the present by singing alleluias when you're tired, discouraged, ill or afraid, or when you simply can't see the way ahead? It has been said that those who sing pray twice.

Come, thou long-expected Jesus,
born to set thy people free.

God for whom we watch and wait,
you sent John the Baptist to prepare the way of your Son:
give us courage to speak the truth,
to hunger for justice,
and to suffer for the cause of right,
with Jesus Christ our Lord.

COLLECT

Monday 23 December

Malachi 1.1, 6-end

'What a weariness this is' (v.13)

The oppressive Babylonian empire didn't last forever. The conquering Persians were far more humane and allowed some of the exiled people of Judah to return to Jerusalem under the leadership of Zerubbabel, grandson of one of the last kings of Judah. But while the exiles returned home with confidence, enthusiastically rebuilding their temple, their long-anticipated prosperity was slow in coming. And there was still no descendant of King David ruling over a new nation.

Disappointment set in. God, they felt, had let them down. And so, while life carried on seemingly 'as normal', there was little enthusiasm and the worship of God became little more than playing at religion.

The prophet Malachi, whose name means 'my messenger' offers a stirring challenge to God's people. His message is clear. If things are not as you think they should be, don't stop worshipping God. Don't blame God. Don't start offering God sacrifices that cost you nothing. Remember how God has been faithful in the past. And keep on keeping on.

How do you cope when you are disappointed? When you feel that God has somehow let you down? When things aren't as you thought they would be? Do you pray less, just go through the motions and offer to God what's left over? If so, you're human like the rest of us! But Malachi's message is clear. We must keep on our toes, pray more not less, and watch for the coming dawn.

COLLECT

God our redeemer,
who prepared the Blessed Virgin Mary
to be the mother of your Son:
grant that, as she looked for his coming as our saviour,
so we may be ready to greet him
when he comes again as our judge;
who is alive and reigns with you,
in the unity of the Holy Spirit,
one God, now and for ever.

Reflection by **Jan McFarlane**

Psalms **45**, 113
Malachi 2.1-16
Matthew 19.13-15

Tuesday 24 December
Christmas Eve

Malachi 2.1-16

'For the lips of a priest should guard knowledge' (v.7)

Malachi turns his attention to the priests, and his words make for uncomfortable reading. God's people have turned away from him in a manner described as akin to adultery. Meanwhile, the priests have been whining and snivelling in the temple because things aren't going their way. Malachi verbally takes them by the shoulders and gives them a good shake and reminds them forcefully of their calling.

Priests, says Malachi, are those who guard the truth. And the people should look to the priests for wisdom and knowledge in matters of faith. How seriously do we take this charge? Sermons and preaching get a bad press and become the butt of jokes perhaps because neither those who preach nor those who listen take this huge responsibility as seriously as we ought. Clergy and lay readers, when did we last make preaching and sermon preparation the most important task of the week? When did we last look seriously at how we preach and ask for honest feedback? And for all of us who listen to sermons, whether they be good or less good, do we approach the task determined to hear what God is saying to us through the preacher?

Today, people will come to our churches who never usually come near. The opportunity to impart something of the truth of the one whose birth we are about to celebrate is a God-given opportunity. How warmly will we welcome them? And how seriously will we take our task?

Almighty God,
you make us glad with the yearly remembrance
of the birth of your Son Jesus Christ:
grant that, as we joyfully receive him as our redeemer,
so we may with sure confidence behold him
when he shall come to be our judge;
who is alive and reigns with you,
in the unity of the Holy Spirit,
one God, now and for ever.

COLLECT

Reflection by **Jan McFarlane**   29

Wednesday 25 December
Christmas Day

Psalms **110,** 117
Isaiah 62.1-5
Matthew 1.18-end

Matthew 1.18-end

'... to fulfil what had been spoken by the Lord through the prophet' (v.22)

Yesterday, we left Malachi's prophesy on the last page of the last book of what Christians know as the Old Testament. Today, we begin with Matthew, the first chapter of the first book of the New Testament. Matthew is our bridge from old to new. Matthew remembers 'what had been spoken by the Lord through the prophet' and, while he refers to Isaiah, we could easily add Malachi and Zephaniah, whose words have accompanied us in our Advent journey towards Christmas Day.

Yesterday, we left Malachi chiding God's people for losing their focus on God and failing to be patient in their long wait for their new warrior-king. Today we celebrate the birth of that king. We know the rest of the story. We know that Jesus won't fulfil the expectations of those who wanted a king to fight for them in earthly terms and who, as a result, will put him to death. We know that he will rise again and, in so doing, widen the meaning of the people of God to include people of every tongue and nation. We know that the long-expected warrior-king will overturn all our expectations by modelling what it means to be a servant-king.

But for today let's be content simply to gaze in wonder at the child in the manger, at the fulfilment of the prophecies, at the miracle of God-with-us, Emmanuel. And resolve once more to follow him to the ends of the earth.

COLLECT

Almighty God,
you have given us your only-begotten Son
to take our nature upon him
and as at this time to be born of a pure virgin:
grant that we, who have been born again
and made your children by adoption and grace,
may daily be renewed by your Holy Spirit;
through Jesus Christ your Son our Lord,
who is alive and reigns with you,
in the unity of the Holy Spirit,
one God, now and for ever.

30   *Reflection by* **Jan McFarlane**

Psalms 13, 31.1-8, 150
Jeremiah 26.12-15
Acts 6

Thursday 26 December
Stephen, deacon, first martyr

Acts 6

'They set up false witnesses' (v.13)

Yesterday, we witnessed the transition from Old Testament to New with the birth of Jesus. Today, we witness another transition and another birth as we read of the events that led up to the conversion of Paul, apostle to the gentiles. And it begins with Stephen.

More accurately, it begins with a squabble. I'm not sure if it's comforting or depressing to know that the first followers of Jesus fell out with each other. Regularly. And often about money, as in the case here where arguments break out about the distribution of the common fund. What's encouraging is that the arguments lead to a positive solution, which involves the commissioning of Stephen as one of the first deacons.

The name Stephen in Greek means 'crown'. Stephen is crowned with faith, grace and authority. He is a compelling witness. Inevitably those who are the greatest witnesses to the gospel become also the greatest targets. False witnesses are set up against Stephen. Many a scholar believes that at the heart of this conspiracy was Saul of Tarsus.

I smile when priests sit in my study and tell me what a hard time they are having. I smile because often it means they are exercising a transformative ministry. How do we deal with opposition? Surely we need first to listen carefully for any element of truth that we need to heed. And then, if the witness proves false, to push forward with confidence and with faith.

Gracious Father,
who gave the first martyr Stephen
grace to pray for those who took up stones against him:
grant that in all our sufferings for the truth
we may learn to love even our enemies
and to seek forgiveness for those who desire our hurt,
looking up to heaven to him who was crucified for us,
Jesus Christ, our mediator and advocate,
who is alive and reigns with you,
in the unity of the Holy Spirit,
one God, now and for ever.

COLLECT

Reflection by **Jan McFarlane**

31

Thursday 27 December
John, Apostle and Evangelist

Psalms **21**, 147.13-end
Exodus 33.12-end
1 John 2.1-11

1 John 2.1-11
'Beloved' (v.7)

'Love changes everything' is a song from the British musical, *Aspects of Love*. It speaks mostly of romantic love and, with its gushing melody, it's a favourite at weddings. Its final line could be a summary of all that John is trying to convey through both his Gospel and his epistles: 'Love will never, never let you be the same'.

The love of which John speaks, the love embodied in Jesus Christ, is transformative. Once we hear ourselves called 'beloved' by the risen Christ, we will never be the same again. God-in-flesh looks at us with love and says, 'be loved'. Once the reality of that love, unearned and undeserved and bought at such a price, really sinks in, it changes everything.

Our actions then need to prove that our lives have been transformed by this mighty power of love. Somehow, we have to show that same love to everyone with no exceptions. Some people are easy to love. Others, let's be honest, are more of a challenge. What does it mean to love them?

Perhaps it means simply trying to see who they are through the lens of God's love for them. Why do they behave as they do? What damage has been done to them in the past? And if we can't manage to walk in their shoes for a while, might we perhaps pray that we might want what's best for them, even if 'love' feels a step too far?

COLLECT

Merciful Lord,
cast your bright beams of light upon the Church:
that, being enlightened by the teaching
of your blessed apostle and evangelist Saint John,
we may so walk in the light of your truth
that we may at last attain to the light of everlasting life;
through Jesus Christ your incarnate Son our Lord,
who is alive and reigns with you,
in the unity of the Holy Spirit,
one God, now and for ever.

Reflection by **Jan McFarlane**

Psalms **36**, 146
Baruch 4.21-27
or Genesis 37.13-20
Matthew 18.1-10

Saturday 28 December
The Holy Innocents

Matthew 18.1-10
'If any of you put a stumbling-block ...' (v.6)

We're told that children in Jesus' day were regarded as of little use until they could replace the adults. Until then, they just needed to be fed and watered, kept alive and largely ignored. Understanding this makes Jesus' words and actions all the more astonishing. Was ever there a less likely candidate for God's kingdom than a snotty-nosed little kid who contributed precisely nothing to the common good? Any fond ideas we may have about earning our place in the kingdom of heaven are swiftly washed away.

I wonder whether Jesus' passionate advocacy for those little ones was a direct result of him learning that all the children in Jerusalem under the age of two had been murdered by King Herod as he sought to destroy the newborn king who might topple him from his throne? Jesus must have known what happened as a result of his birth. I can't believe that his heart wasn't torn asunder with sorrow and with anger.

Jesus is very clear about what awaits anyone who harms children. You can almost hear the controlled anger in his voice. And lest we move on, thinking we've never harmed a child, it might be worth us considering what it means to put a stumbling-block in their way. For as the followers of one who placed little ones at the heart of the kingdom, is it not odd that so many of our churches are empty of children?

Heavenly Father,
whose children suffered at the hands of Herod,
though they had done no wrong:
by the suffering of your Son
and by the innocence of our lives
frustrate all evil designs
and establish your reign of justice and peace;
through Jesus Christ your Son our Lord,
who is alive and reigns with you,
in the unity of the Holy Spirit,
one God, now and for ever.

COLLECT

Reflection by **Jan McFarlane**   33

Morning Prayer – a simple form

O Lord, open our lips
and our mouth shall proclaim your praise.

A prayer of thanksgiving for Advent

Blessed are you, Sovereign God of all,
to you be praise and glory for ever.
In your tender compassion
the dawn from on high is breaking upon us
to dispel the lingering shadows of night.
As we look for your coming among us this day,
open our eyes to behold your presence
and strengthen our hands to do your will,
that the world may rejoice and give you praise.
Blessed be God, Father, Son and Holy Spirit.
Blessed be God for ever.

Word of God

Psalmody *(the psalm or psalms listed for the day)*

**Glory to the Father and to the Son
and to the Holy Spirit;
as it was in the beginning is now:
and shall be for ever. Amen.**

Reading from Holy Scripture *(one or both of the passages set for the day)*

Reflection

The Benedictus (The Song of Zechariah) *(see opposite page)*

Prayers

Intercessions – a time of prayer for the day and its tasks, the world and its need, the church and her life.

The Collect for the Day

The Lord's Prayer *(see p. 37)*

Conclusion

A blessing or the Grace *(see p. 37),* or a concluding response

Let us bless the Lord
Thanks be to God

Benedictus (The Song of Zechariah)

1   Blessed be the Lord the God of Israel, ♦
    who has come to his people and set them free.

2   He has raised up for us a mighty Saviour, ♦
    born of the house of his servant David.

3   Through his holy prophets God promised of old ♦
    to save us from our enemies,
        from the hands of all that hate us,

4   To show mercy to our ancestors, ♦
    and to remember his holy covenant.

5   This was the oath God swore to our father Abraham: ♦
    to set us free from the hands of our enemies,

6   Free to worship him without fear, ♦
    holy and righteous in his sight
        all the days of our life.

7   And you, child, shall be called the prophet of the Most High, ♦
    for you will go before the Lord to prepare his way,

8   To give his people knowledge of salvation ♦
    by the forgiveness of all their sins.

9   In the tender compassion of our God ♦
    the dawn from on high shall break upon us,

10 To shine on those who dwell in darkness
        and the shadow of death, ♦
    and to guide our feet into the way of peace.

Luke 1.68-79

**Glory to the Father and to the Son
and to the Holy Spirit;
as it was in the beginning is now:
and shall be for ever. Amen.**

Seasonal Prayers of Thanksgiving

Blessed are you, Sovereign God of all,
to you be praise and glory for ever.
In your tender compassion
the dawn from on high is breaking upon us
to dispel the lingering shadows of night.
As we look for your coming among us this day,
open our eyes to behold your presence
and strengthen our hands to do your will,
that the world may rejoice and give you praise.
Blessed be God, Father, Son and Holy Spirit.
Blessed be God for ever.

At Any Time

Blessed are you, creator of all,
to you be praise and glory for ever.
As your dawn renews the face of the earth
bringing light and life to all creation,
may we rejoice in this day you have made;
as we wake refreshed from the depths of sleep,
open our eyes to behold your presence
and strengthen our hands to do your will,
that the world may rejoice and give you praise.
Blessed be God, Father, Son and Holy Spirit.
Blessed be God for ever.

after Lancelot Andrewes (1626)

The Lord's Prayer and The Grace

Our Father in heaven,
hallowed be your name,
your kingdom come,
your will be done,
on earth as in heaven.
Give us today our daily bread.
Forgive us our sins
as we forgive those who sin against us.
Lead us not into temptation
but deliver us from evil.
For the kingdom, the power,
and the glory are yours
now and for ever.
Amen.

(or)

Our Father, who art in heaven,
hallowed be thy name;
thy kingdom come;
thy will be done;
on earth as it is in heaven.
Give us this day our daily bread.
And forgive us our trespasses,
as we forgive those who trespass against us.
And lead us not into temptation;
but deliver us from evil.
For thine is the kingdom,
the power and the glory,
for ever and ever.
Amen.

The grace of our Lord Jesus Christ,
and the love of God,
and the fellowship of the Holy Spirit,
be with us all evermore.
Amen.

An Order for Night Prayer (Compline)

The Lord almighty grant us a quiet night and a perfect end.
Amen.

Our help is in the name of the Lord
who made heaven and earth.

A period of silence for reflection on the past day may follow.

The following or other suitable words of penitence may be used

**Most merciful God,
we confess to you,
before the whole company of heaven and one another,
that we have sinned in thought, word and deed
and in what we have failed to do.
Forgive us our sins,
heal us by your Spirit
and raise us to new life in Christ. Amen.**

O God, make speed to save us.
O Lord, make haste to help us.

**Glory to the Father and to the Son
and to the Holy Spirit;
as it was in the beginning is now
and shall be for ever. Amen.
Alleluia.**

The following or another suitable hymn may be sung

Before the ending of the day,
Creator of the world, we pray
That you, with steadfast love, would keep
Your watch around us while we sleep.

From evil dreams defend our sight,
From fears and terrors of the night;
Tread underfoot our deadly foe
That we no sinful thought may know.

O Father, that we ask be done
Through Jesus Christ, your only Son;
And Holy Spirit, by whose breath
Our souls are raised to life from death.

The Word of God

One or more of Psalms 4, 91 or 134 may be used.

Psalm 134

1   Come, bless the Lord, all you servants of the Lord, ♦
     you that by night stand in the house of the Lord.

2   Lift up your hands towards the sanctuary ♦
     and bless the Lord.

3   The Lord who made heaven and earth ♦
     give you blessing out of Zion.

**Glory to the Father and to the Son
and to the Holy Spirit;
as it was in the beginning is now
and shall be for ever. Amen.**

Scripture Reading

*One of the following short lessons or another suitable
passage is read*

You, O Lord, are in the midst of us and we are called by your
name; leave us not, O Lord our God.

Jeremiah 14.9

(or)

Be sober, be vigilant, because your adversary the devil is
prowling round like a roaring lion, seeking for someone
to devour. Resist him, strong in the faith.

1 Peter 5.8,9

(or)

The servants of the Lamb shall see the face of God, whose name
will be on their foreheads. There will be no more night: they will
not need the light of a lamp or the light of the sun, for God will
be their light, and they will reign for ever and ever.

Revelation 22.4,5

The following responsory may be said

Into your hands, O Lord, I commend my spirit.
Into your hands, O Lord, I commend my spirit.
For you have redeemed me, Lord God of truth.
I commend my spirit.
Glory to the Father and to the Son
and to the Holy Spirit.
Into your hands, O Lord, I commend my spirit.

Or, in Easter

Into your hands, O Lord, I commend my spirit.
    Alleluia, alleluia.
Into your hands, O Lord, I commend my spirit.
    Alleluia, alleluia.
For you have redeemed me, Lord God of truth.
Alleluia, alleluia.
Glory to the Father and to the Son
and to the Holy Spirit.
Into your hands, O Lord, I commend my spirit.
    Alleluia, alleluia.

Keep me as the apple of your eye.
Hide me under the shadow of your wings.

Gospel Canticle

Nunc Dimittis (The Song of Simeon)

Save us, O Lord, while waking,
and guard us while sleeping,
that awake we may watch with Christ
and asleep may rest in peace.

1   Now, Lord, you let your servant go in peace:
    your word has been fulfilled.

2   My own eyes have seen the salvation
    which you have prepared in the sight of every people;

3   A light to reveal you to the nations
    and the glory of your people Israel.

Luke 2.29-32

Glory to the Father and to the Son
and to the Holy Spirit;
as it was in the beginning is now
and shall be for ever. Amen.

Save us, O Lord, while waking,
and guard us while sleeping,
that awake we may watch with Christ
and asleep may rest in peace.

Prayers

Intercessions and thanksgivings may be offered here.

The Collect

Visit this place, O Lord, we pray,
and drive far from it the snares of the enemy;
may your holy angels dwell with us and guard us in peace,
and may your blessing be always upon us;
through Jesus Christ our Lord.
Amen.

The Lord's Prayer (see p. 37) may be said.

The Conclusion

In peace we will lie down and sleep;
for you alone, Lord, make us dwell in safety.

Abide with us, Lord Jesus,
for the night is at hand and the day is now past.

As the night watch looks for the morning,
so do we look for you, O Christ.

[Come with the dawning of the day
and make yourself known in the breaking of the bread.]

The Lord bless us and watch over us;
the Lord make his face shine upon us and be gracious to us;
the Lord look kindly on us and give us peace.
Amen.

Love what you've read?

Why not consider using *Reflections for Daily Prayer* all year round? We also publish these Bible reflections in an annual format, containing material for the entire Church year.

The volume for the **2019/20** Church year is now available and features contributions from a host of distinguished writers: Rosalind Brown, Vanessa Conant, Gillian Cooper, Steven Croft, Alan Everett, Marcus Green, Malcolm Guite, Christopher Herbert, Tricia Hillas, Michael Ipgrave, John Kiddle, Jan McFarlane, Jessica Martin, Julia Mourant, Martyn Percy, John Pritchard, Brother Samuel SSF, Angela Tilby and Lucy Winkett.

REFLECTIONS FOR DAILY PRAYER
Advent 2019 to the eve of Advent 2020

ISBN 978 1 78140 123 1   **£16.99** • 336 pages

Please note: this book reproduces the material for Advent found in the volume you are now holding.

Reflections for Daily Prayer **2020/21** will be available from May 2020 with reflections written by: Kate Bruce, Richard Carter, Andrew Davison, Guli Francis-Dehqani, Peter Graystone, Liz Hoare, Michael Ipgrave, Graham James, Donna Lazenby, Anna Matthews, Barbara Mosse, Mark Oakley, Sue Pickering, Ben Quash, Sarah Rowland Jones, David Runcorn, Meg Warner, Margaret Whipp and Jeremy Worthen.

REFLECTIONS FOR DAILY PRAYER
Advent 2020 to the eve of Advent 2021

ISBN 978 1 78140 179 8   **£16.99** • 336 pages

REFLECTIONS FOR SUNDAYS (YEAR A)

Reflections for Sundays offers over 250 reflections on the Principal Readings for every Sunday and major Holy Day in Year A, from the same experienced team of writers that have made *Reflections for Daily Prayer* so successful. For each Sunday and major Holy Day, they provide:

- full lectionary details for the Principal Service
- a reflection on each Old Testament reading (both Continuous and Related)
- a reflection on the Epistle
- a reflection on the Gospel.

This book also contains a substantial introduction to the Gospel of Matthew, written by Paula Gooder.

£14.99 • 288 pages
ISBN 978 0 7151 4735 1

Also available in Kindle and epub formats

REFLECTIONS ON THE PSALMS

£14.99 • 192 pages
ISBN 978 0 7151 4490 9

Reflections on the Psalms provides original and insightful meditations on each of the Bible's 150 Psalms.

Each reflection is accompanied by its corresponding Psalm refrain and prayer from the *Common Worship Psalter*, making this a valuable resource for personal or devotional use.

Specially written introductions by Paula Gooder and Steven Croft explore the Psalms and the Bible and the Psalms in the life of the Church.

REFLECTIONS FOR DAILY PRAYER
App

Make Bible study and reflection a part of your routine wherever you go with the Reflections for Daily Prayer App for Apple and Android devices.

Download the app for free from the App Store (Apple devices) or Google Play (Android devices) and receive a week's worth of reflections free. Then purchase a monthly, three-monthly or annual subscription to receive up-to-date content.